A PRAYER FOR THE
ANIMALS

Daniel Kirk

ABRAMS BOOKS FOR YOUNG READERS, NEW YORK

May all the animals
of the earth,

and the animals of the sky,

and the animals of the sea

be at peace.

May they be **free** of hunger, may they be **free** of fear,

and may their hearts and minds be calm.

May everything in their world

be just as it was meant to be.

May the animals of the earth feel **safe** and **secure**:

wild animals, working animals, and pets alike.

May all of their needs be met

so that they can enjoy

the gentle b r e e z e,

or the shining moon and stars,
or the chill of night,

or the dark and hidden places,

if that is their beloved home.

May all of the animals
be at rest.

May our hearts be open to caring
for the animals of this world,

to being a friend, a protector of the big and the small,

that they might have the things

we wish for ourselves . . . . good things to eat,

a safe place to live,

and the companionship

of friends and family,

all the days of their lives.

Author's Note

People around the world observe World Animal Day on October 4 or participate in the Blessing of the Animals—associated with Saint Francis of Assisi, patron saint of animals—as a chance to celebrate our love for the animals in our lives. The trust and loyalty between humans and our animal friends is something very special, bringing meaning and purpose to our lives and teaching us about caring for others. In my career as an artist and writer, I have often used animals to tell stories of friendship and love. Everyone can show our care and concern for animals by celebrating World Animal Day. Animal shelters and animal rights organizations always appreciate volunteers and donations of money, blankets, and food. And our animal companions will love the extra attention and time we spend with them!

For Ivy, Raleigh, and Russell, animal lovers all

The illustrations in this book were made in pencil, colored in Photoshop.

Cataloging-in-Publication Data has been applied for and may be obtained from the Library of Congress.

ISBN 978-1-4197-3199-0

Text and illustrations copyright © 2018 Daniel Kirk
Book design by Julia Marvel

Printed and bound in China
10 9 8 7 6 5 4 3 2 1

Abrams Books for Young Readers are available at special discounts when purchased in quantity for premiums and promotions as well as fundraising or educational use. Special editions can also be created to specification. For details, contact specialsales@abramsbooks.com or the address below.

ABRAMS The Art of Books
195 Broadway, New York, NY 10007
abramsbooks.com